ALPACA
COLORING BOOK

ART THERAPY

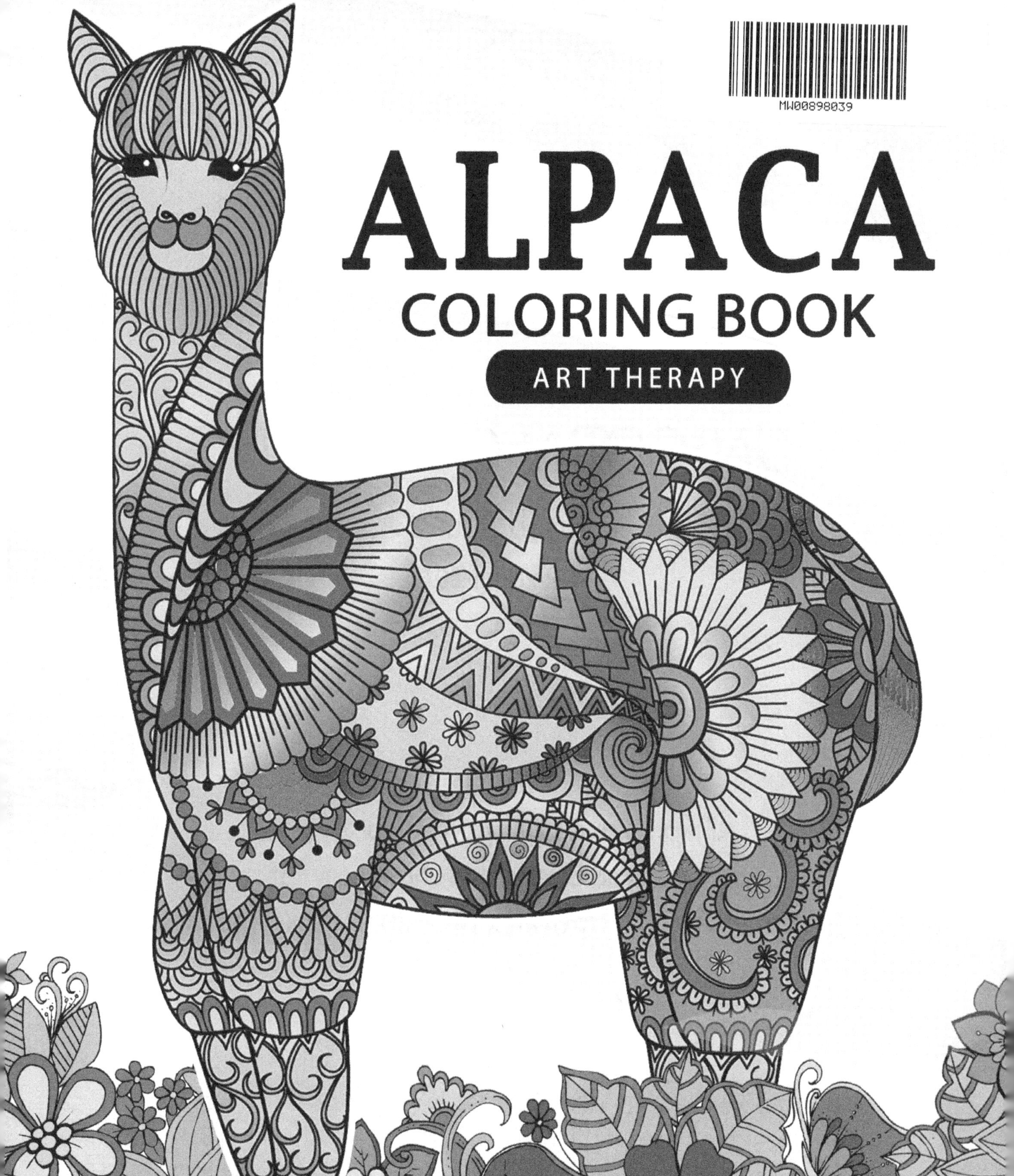

STRESS RELIEVING

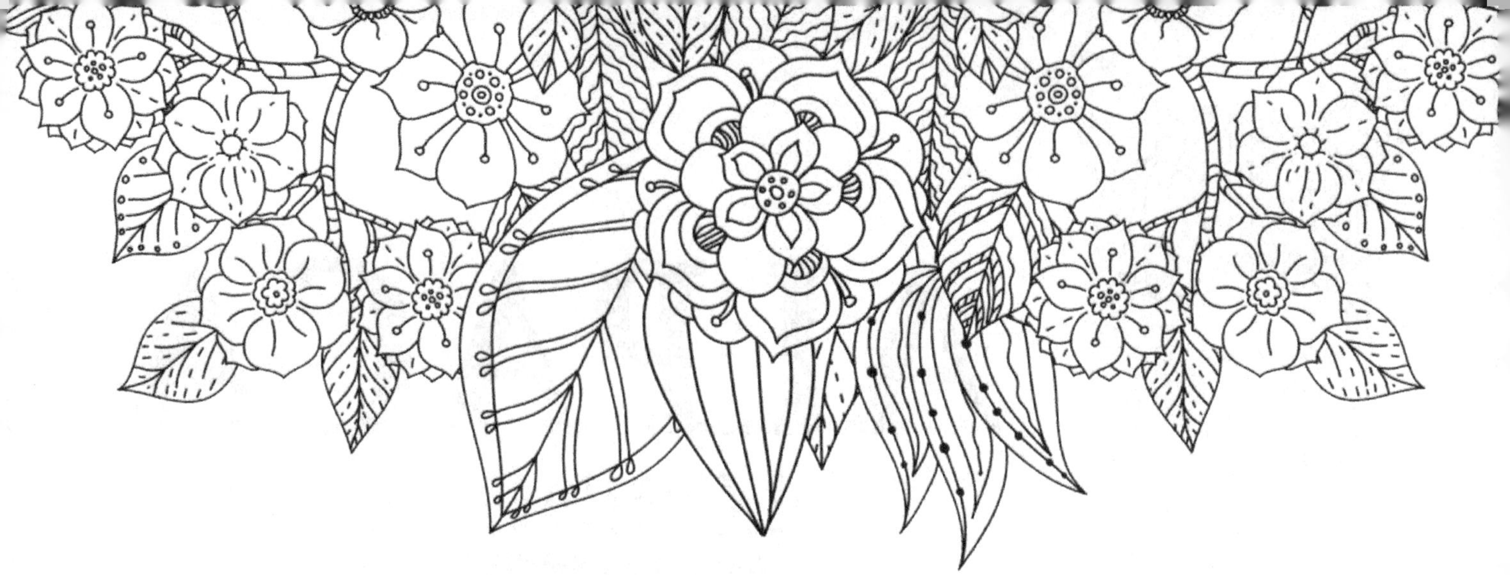

UNICORN COLORING

Printed in U.S.A.

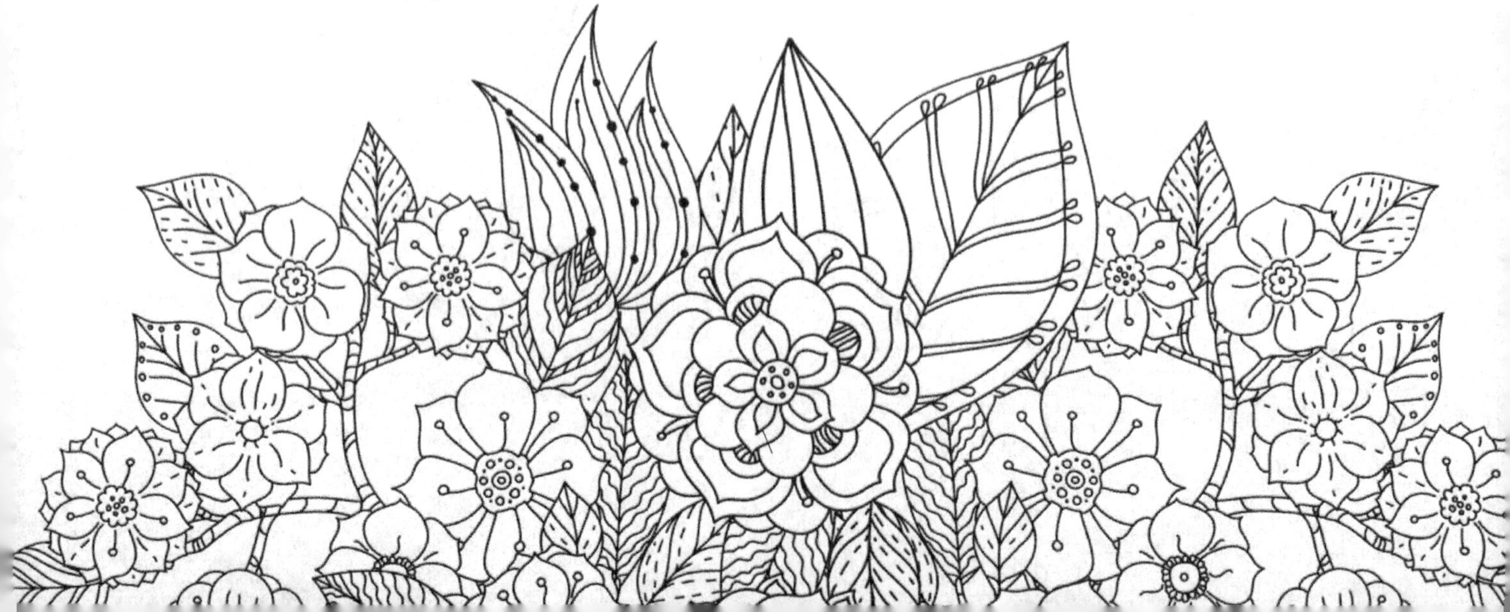

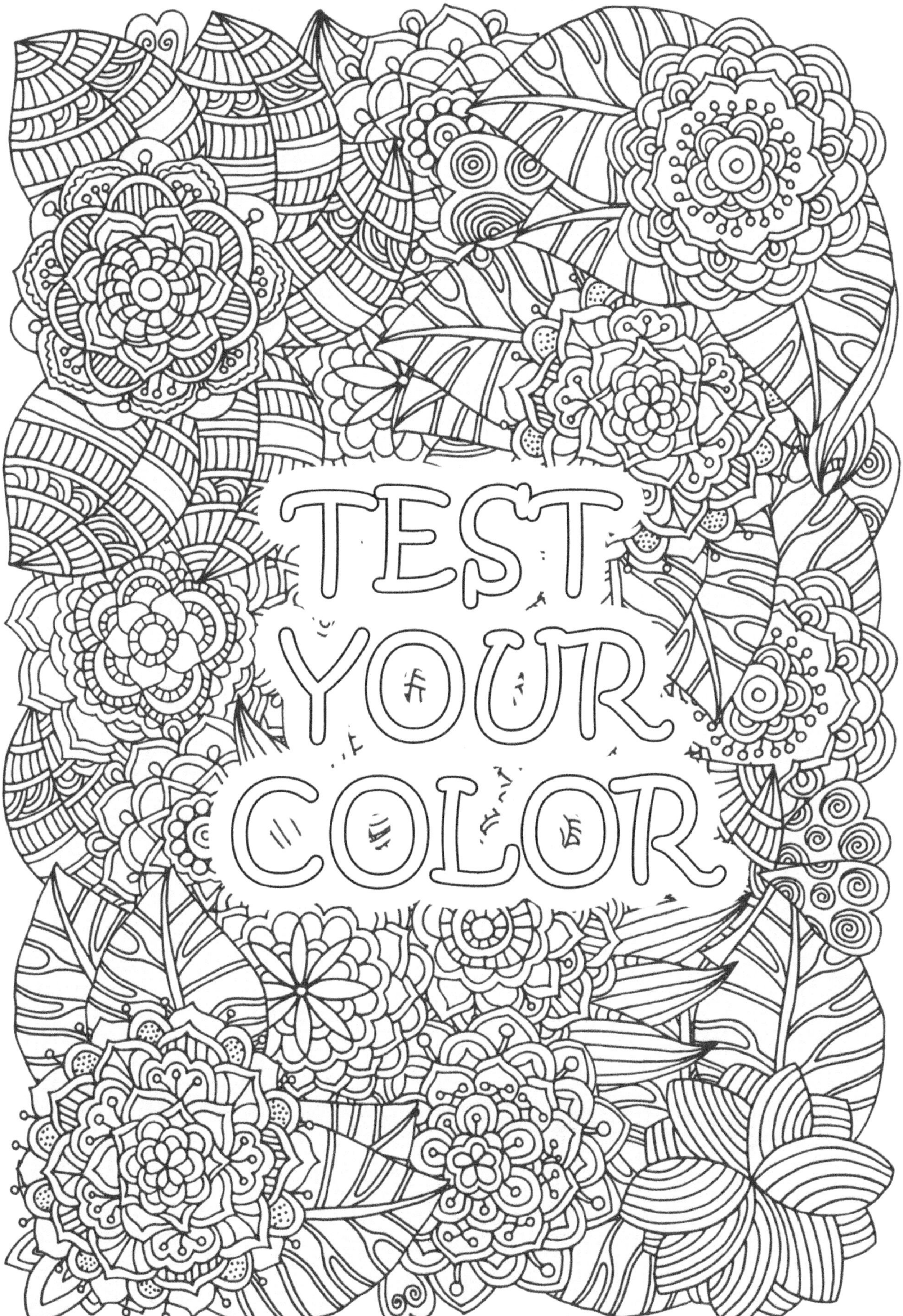
TEST
YOUR
COLOR

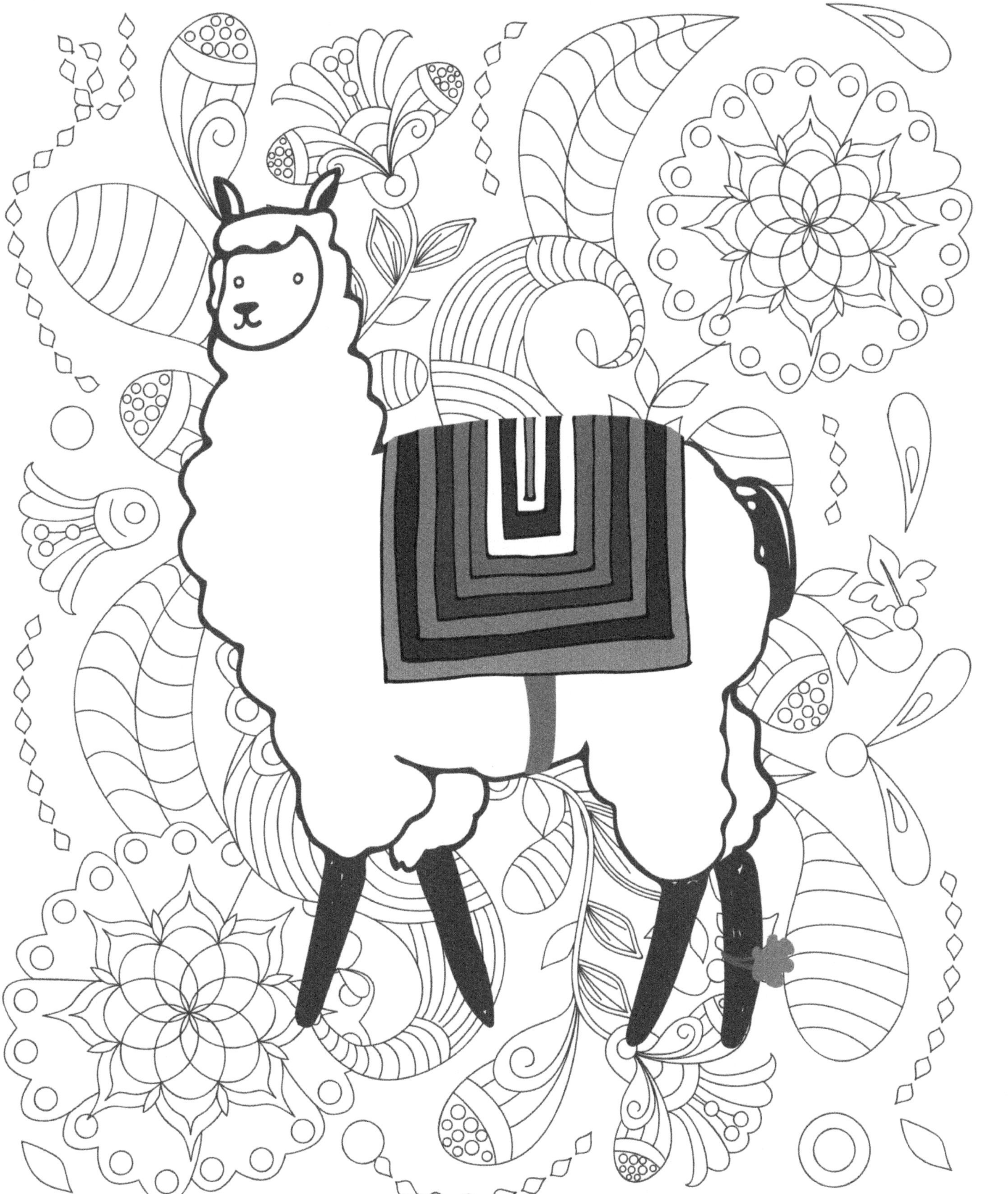

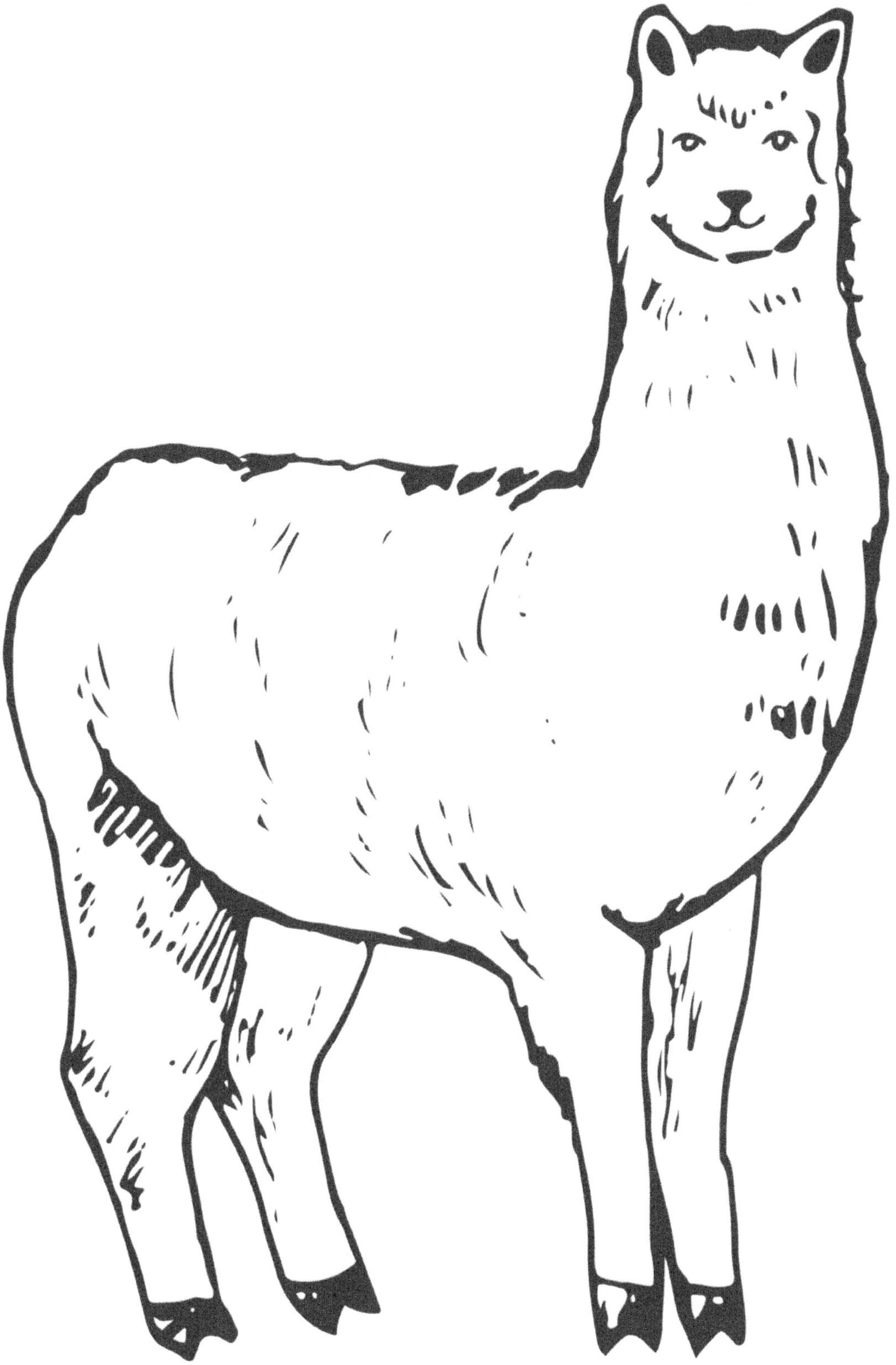

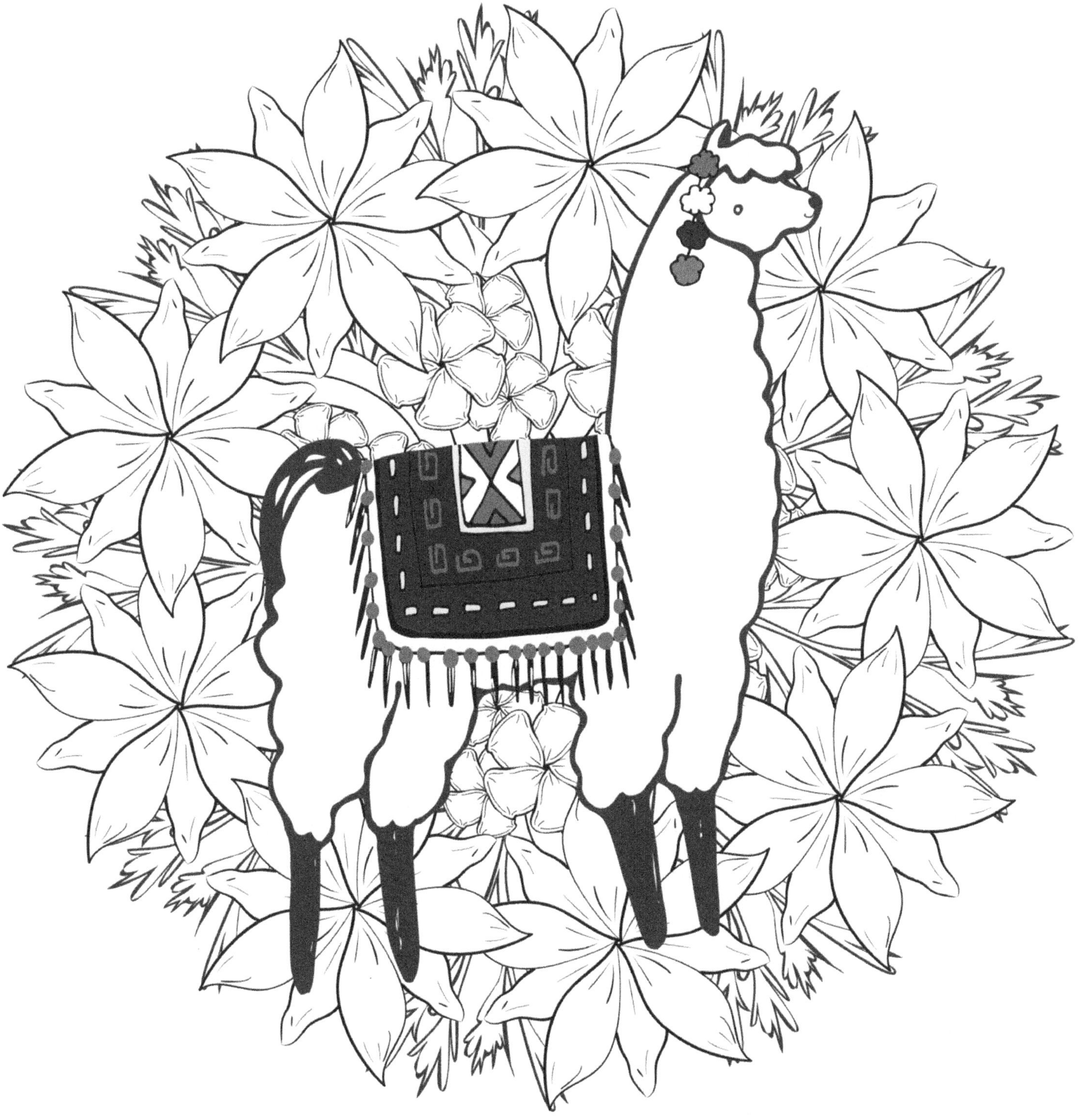

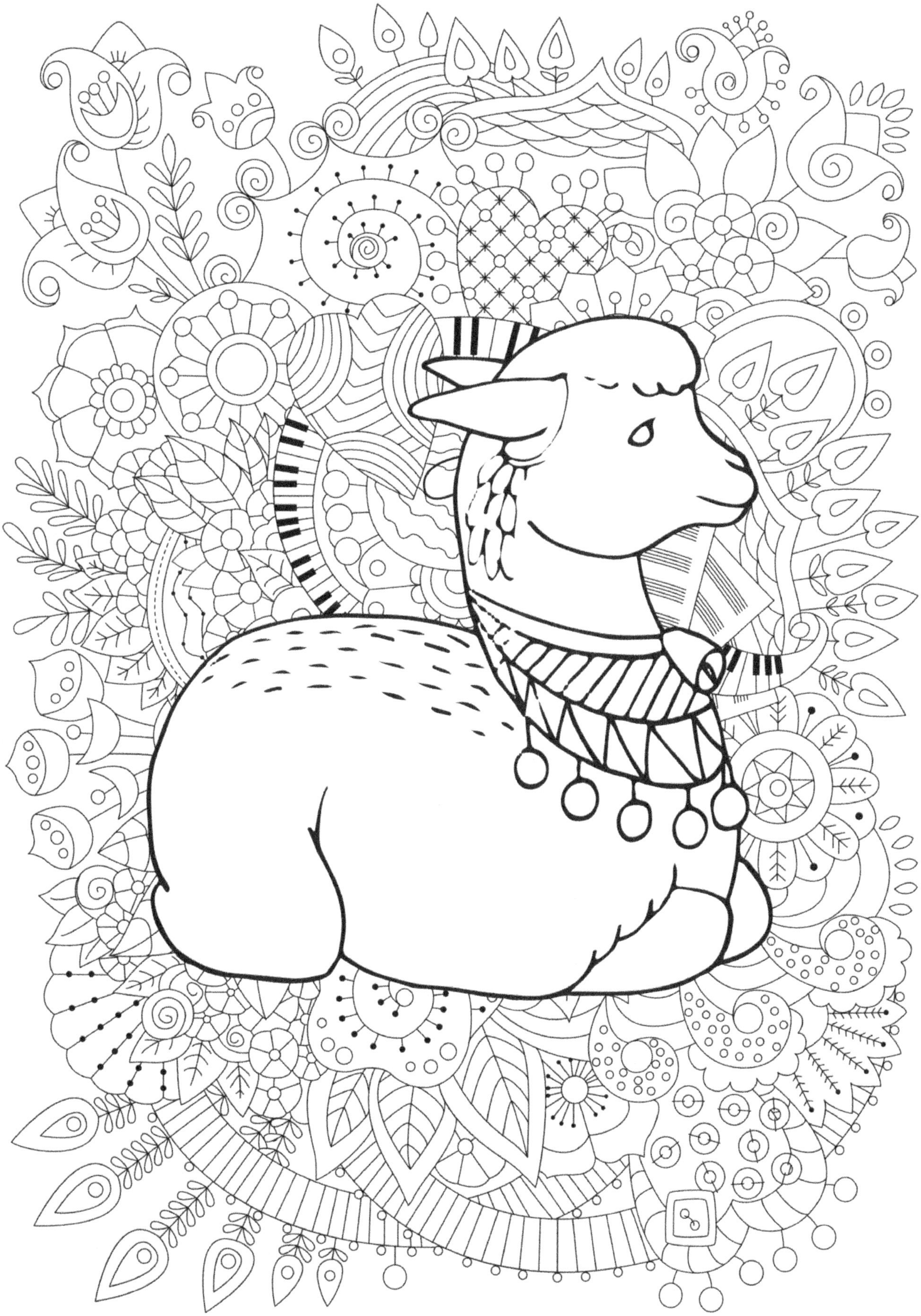

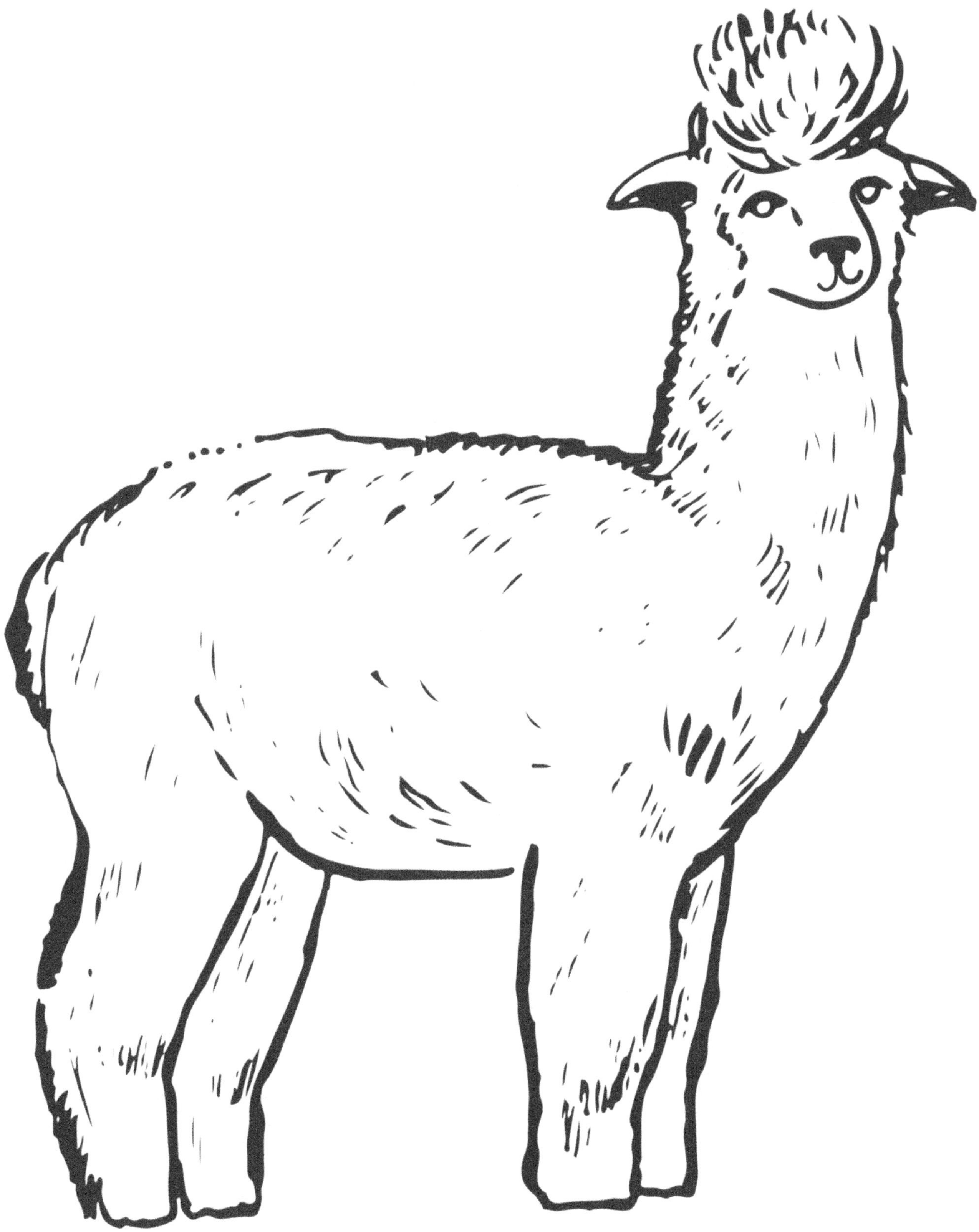

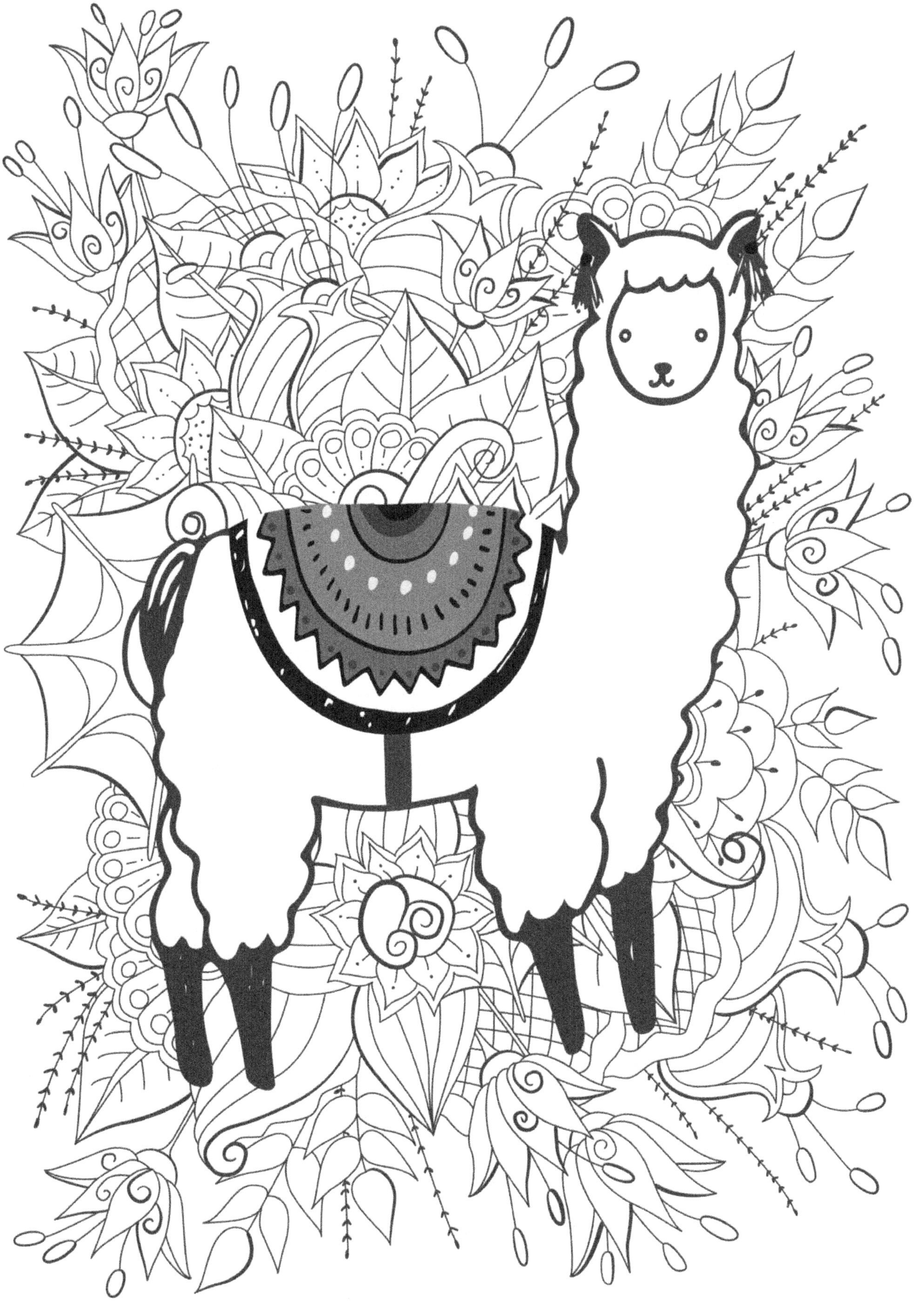

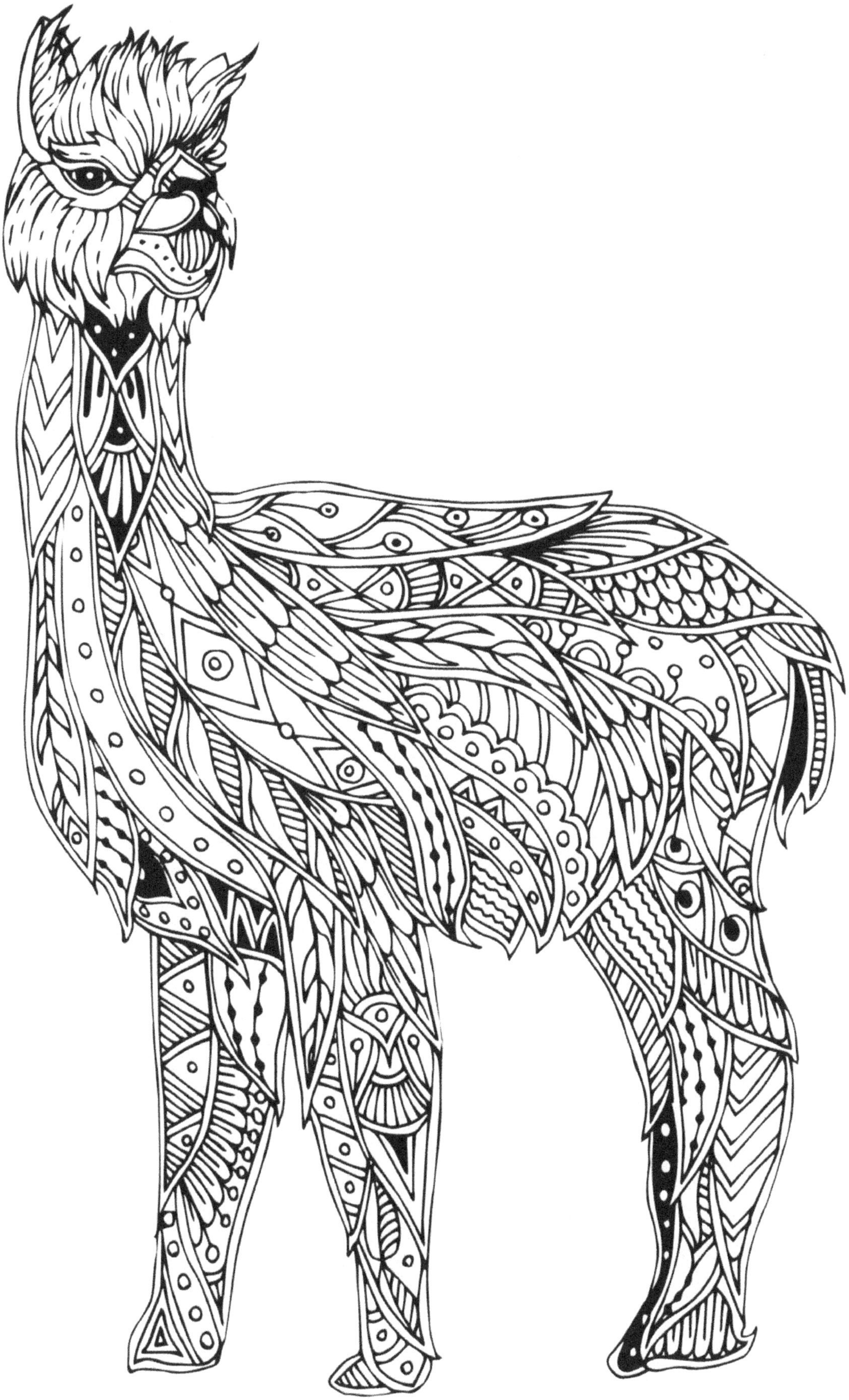

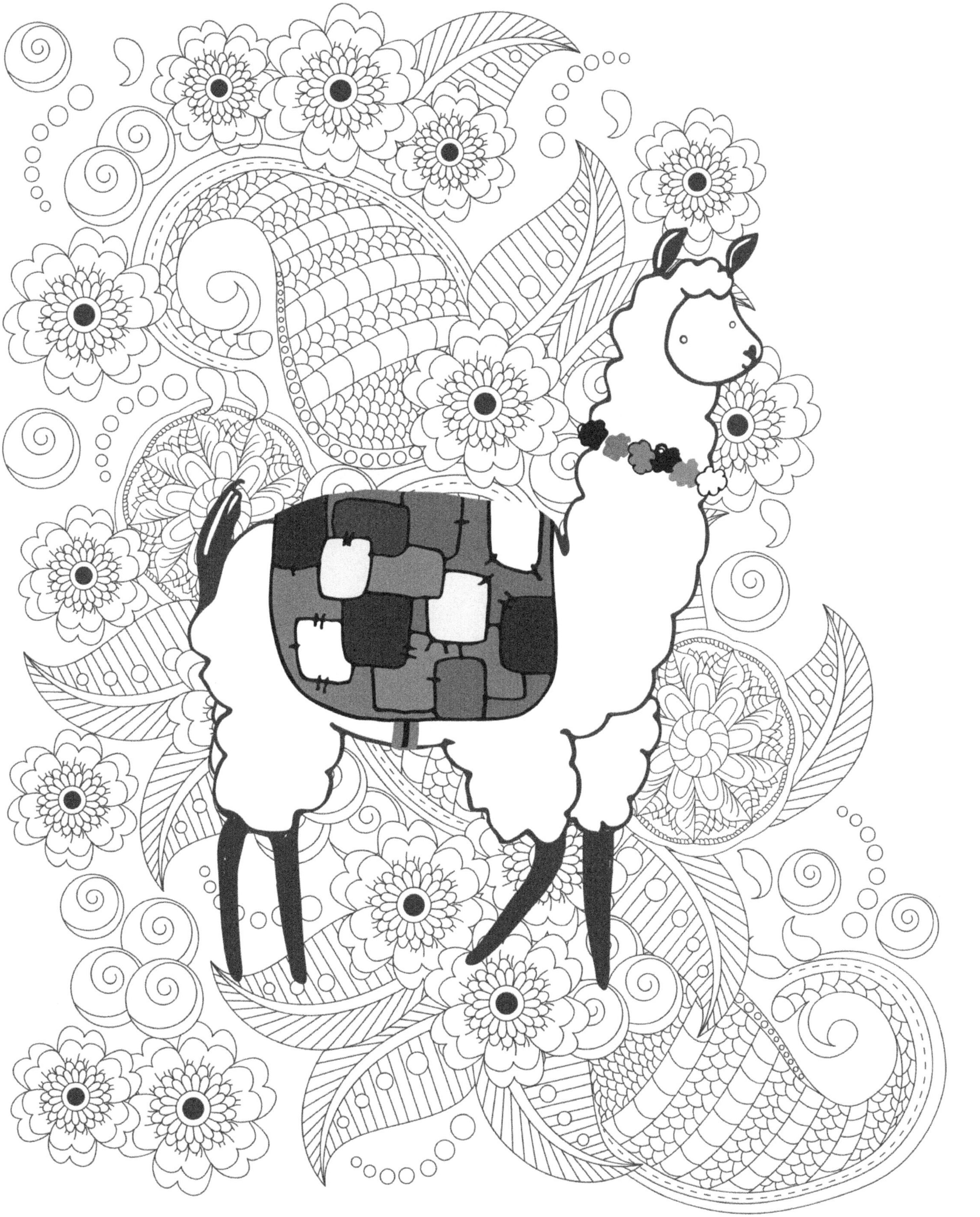

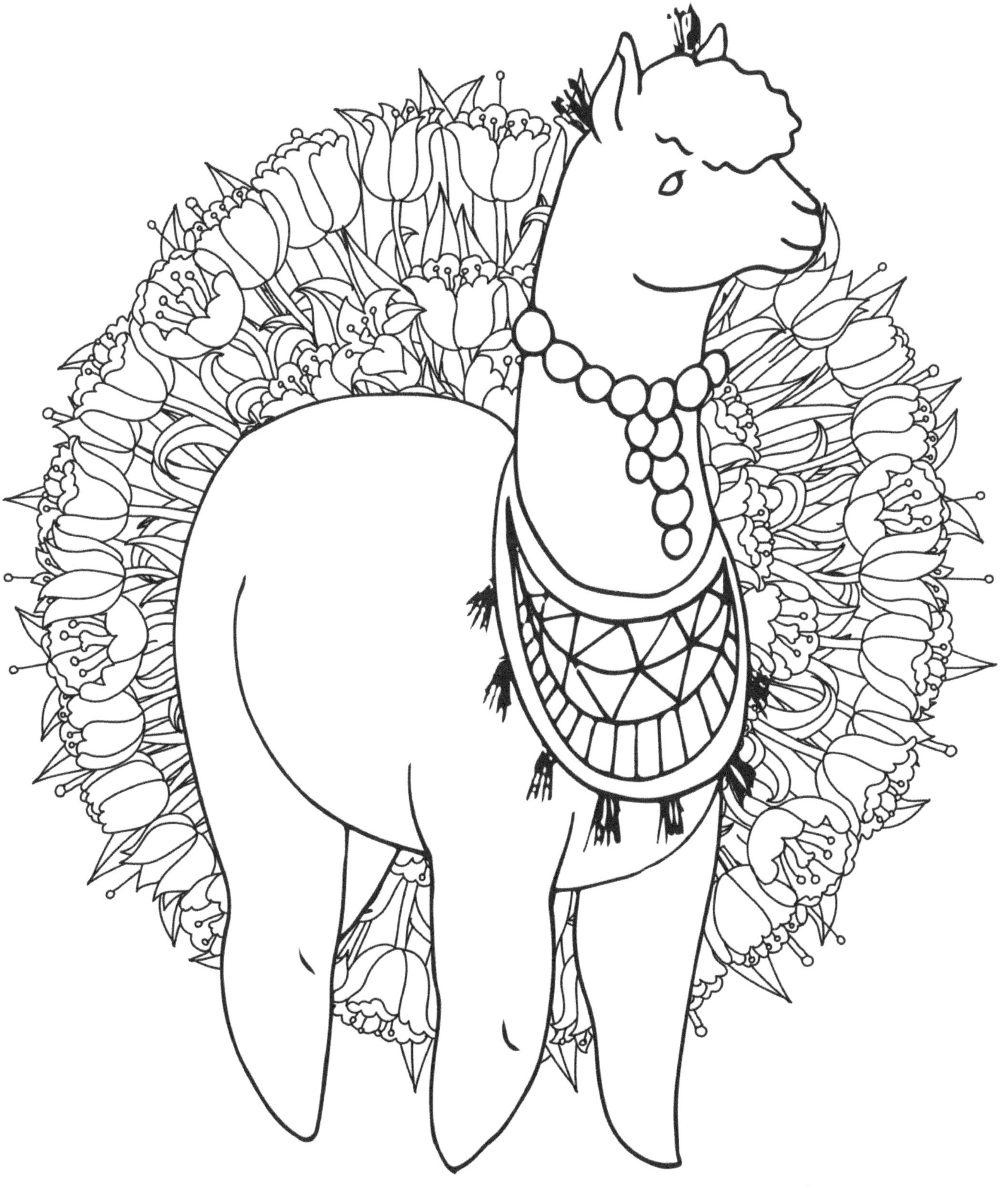

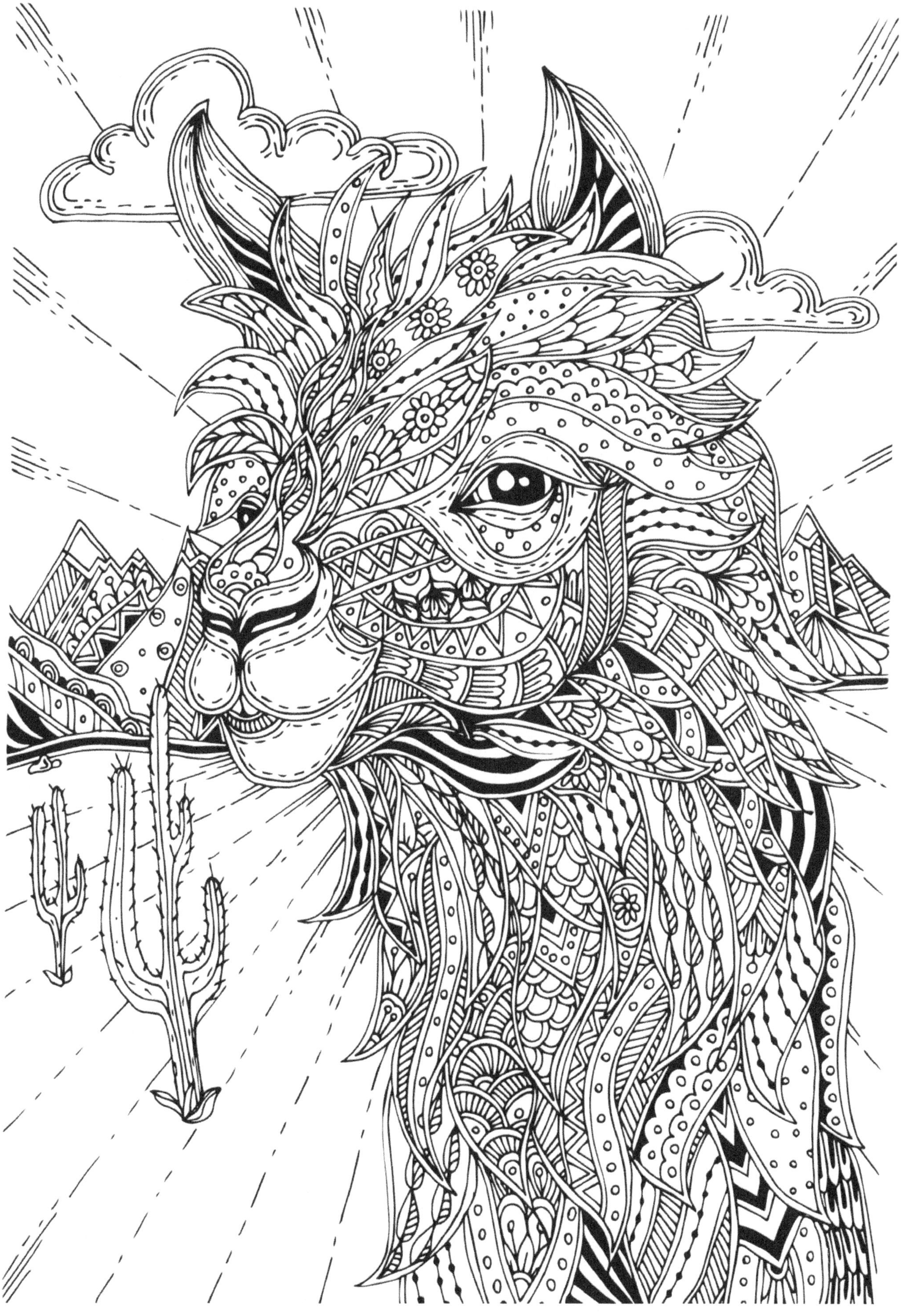

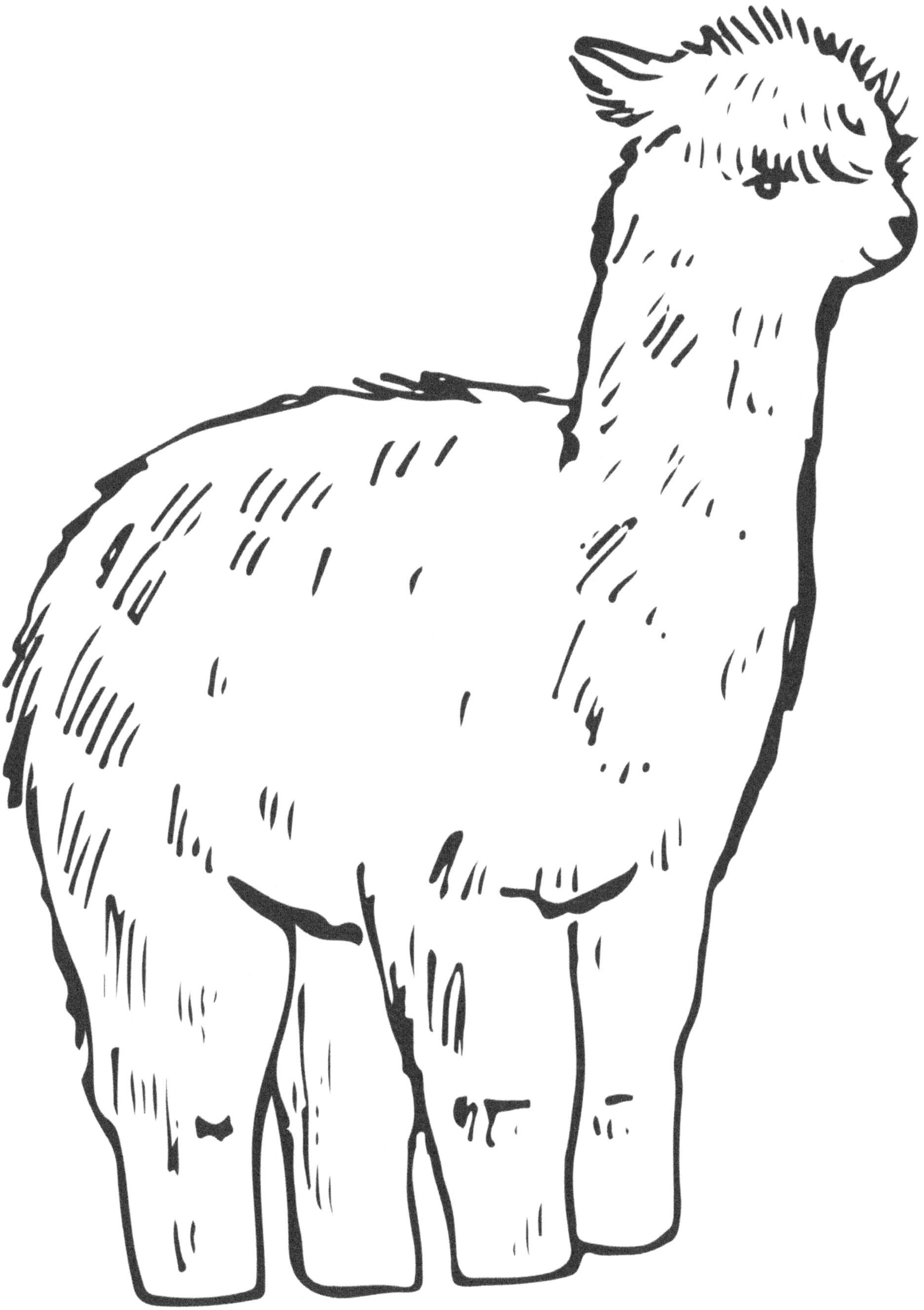

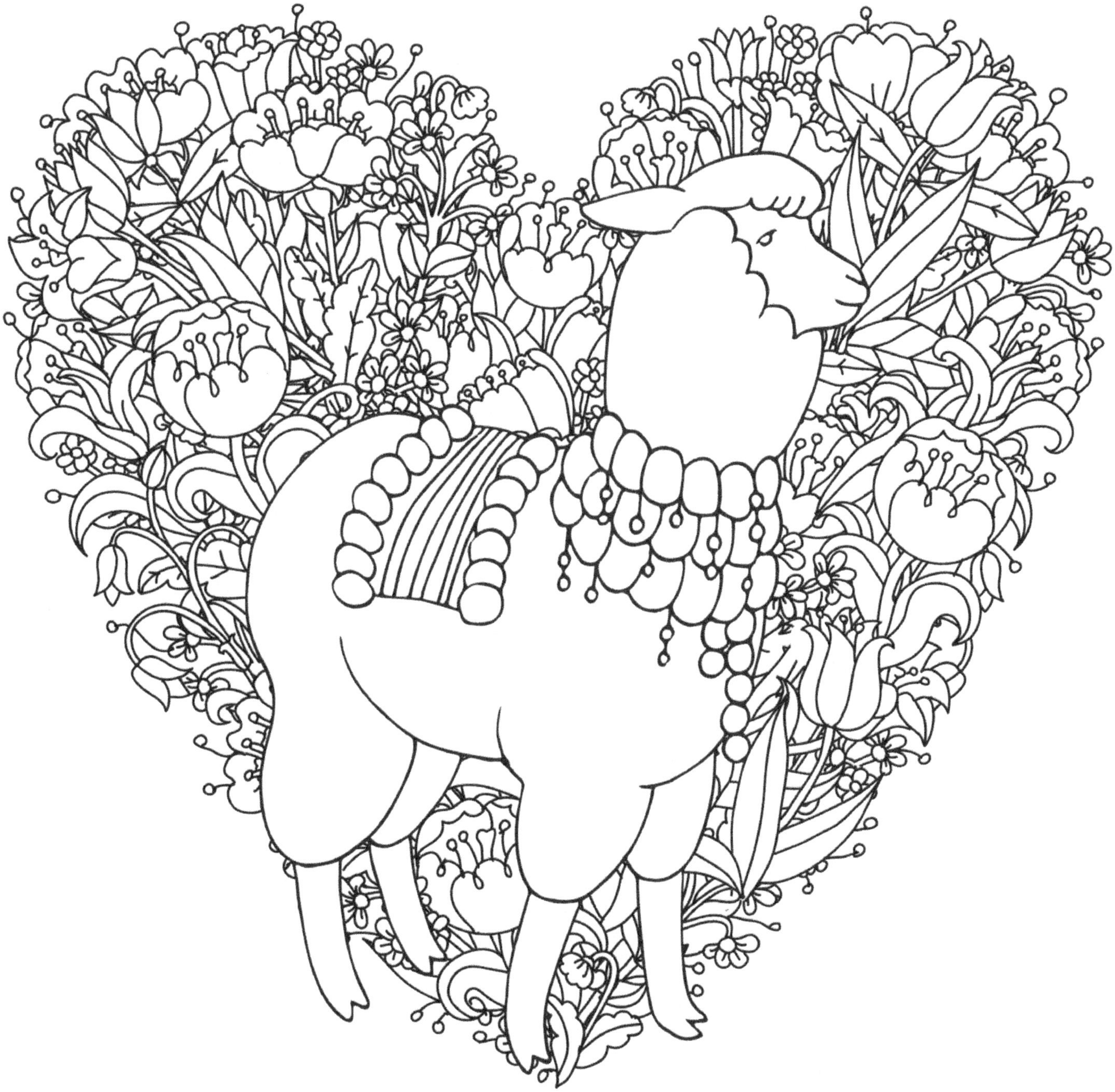

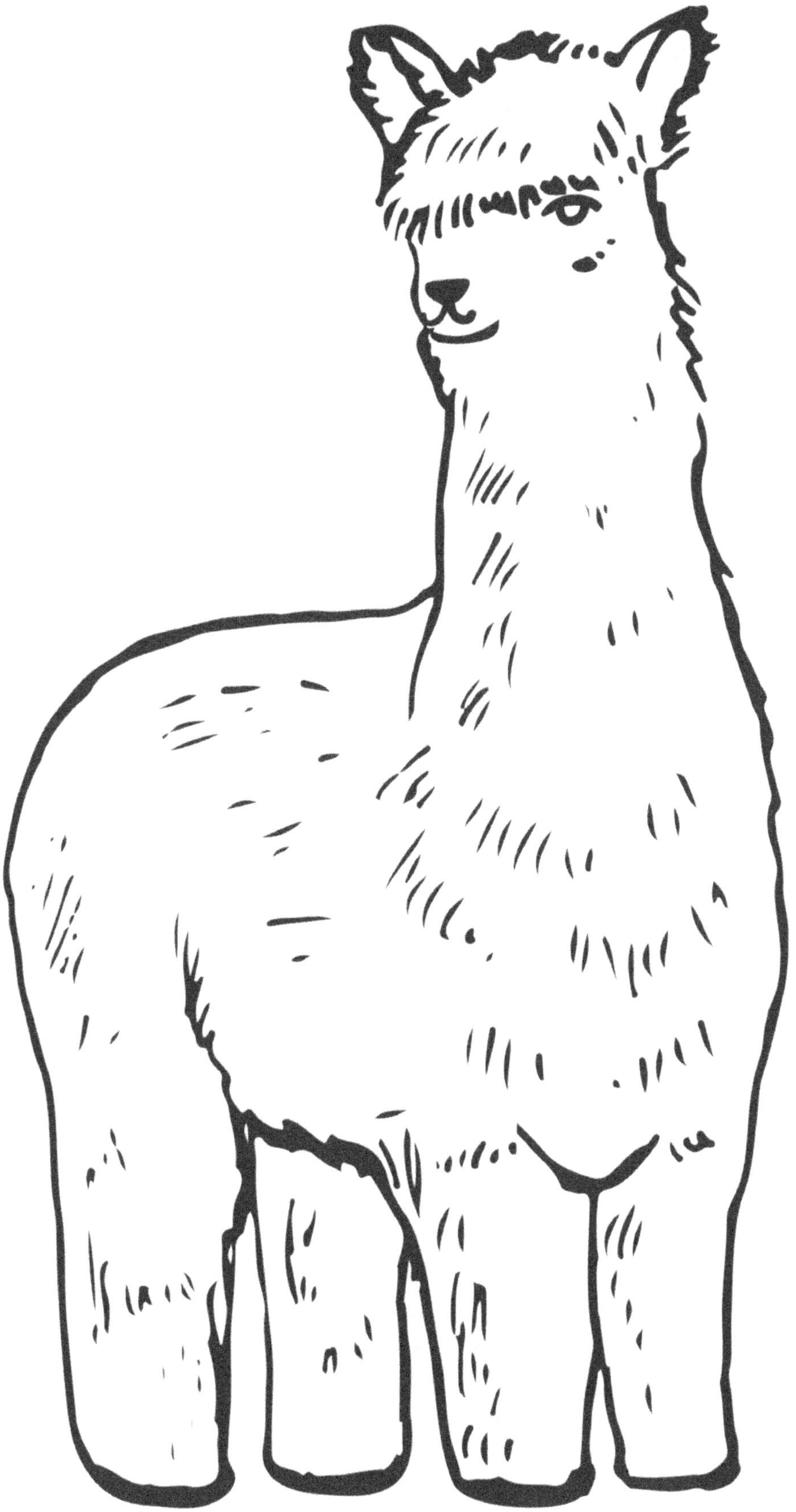

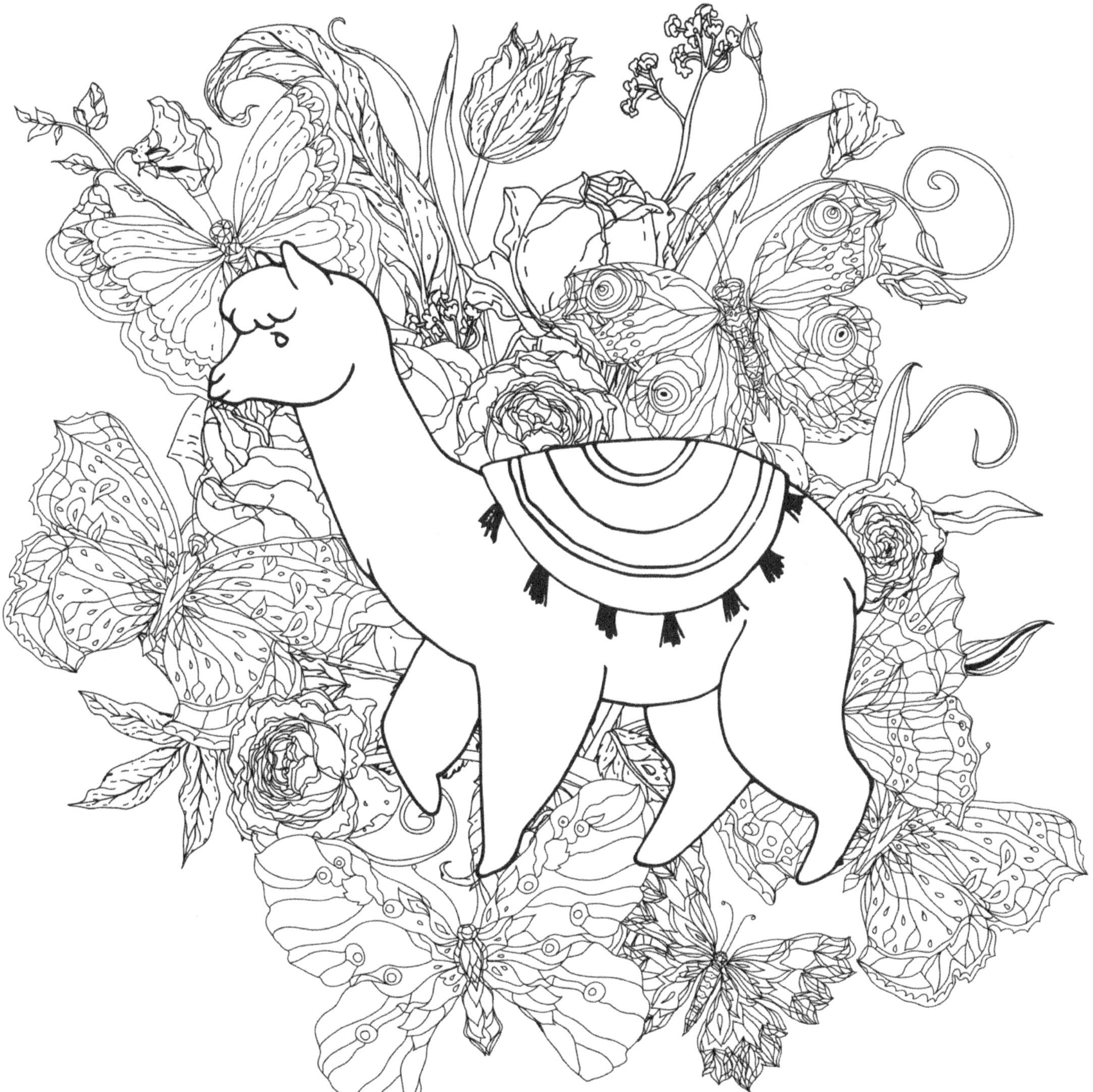

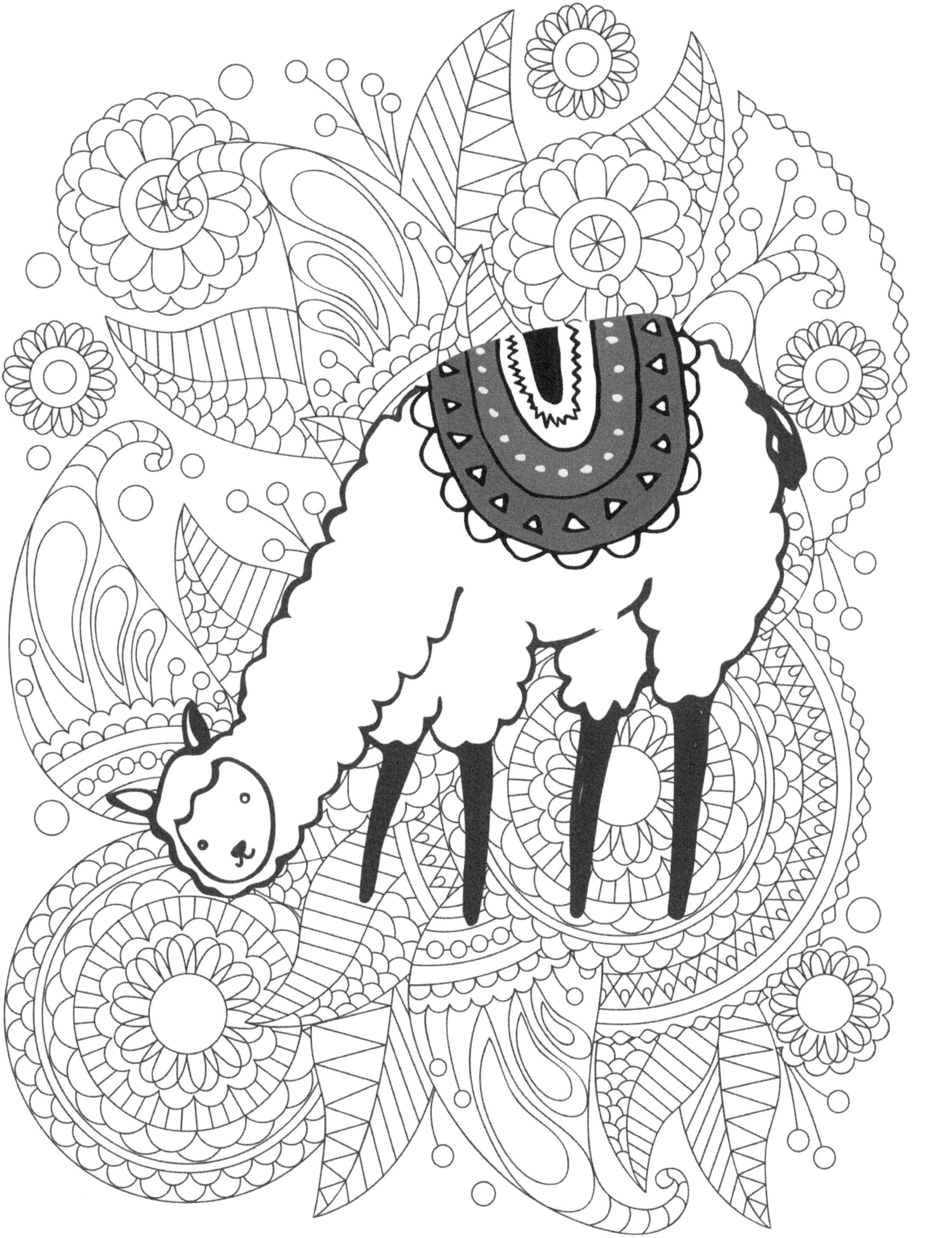

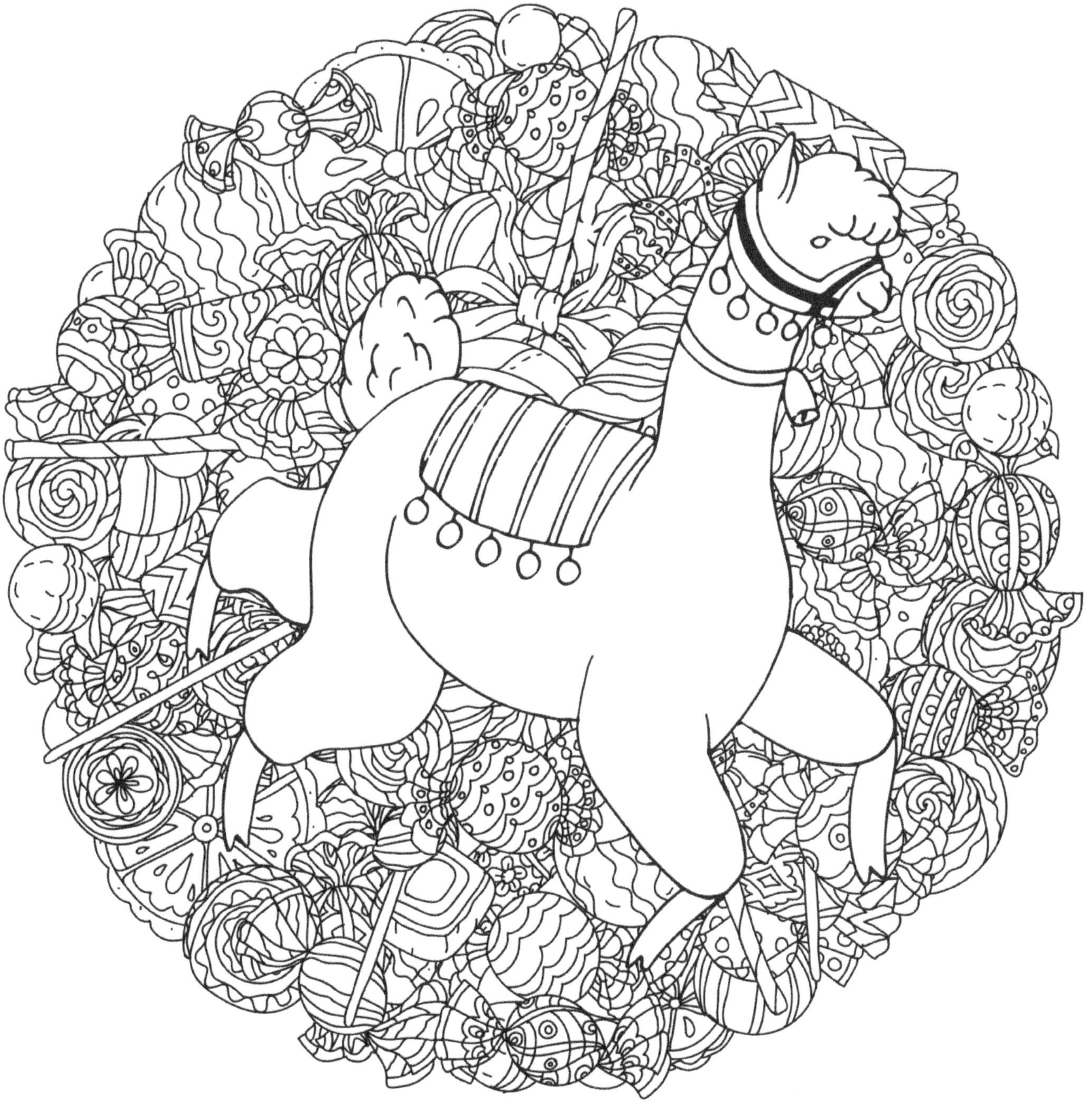

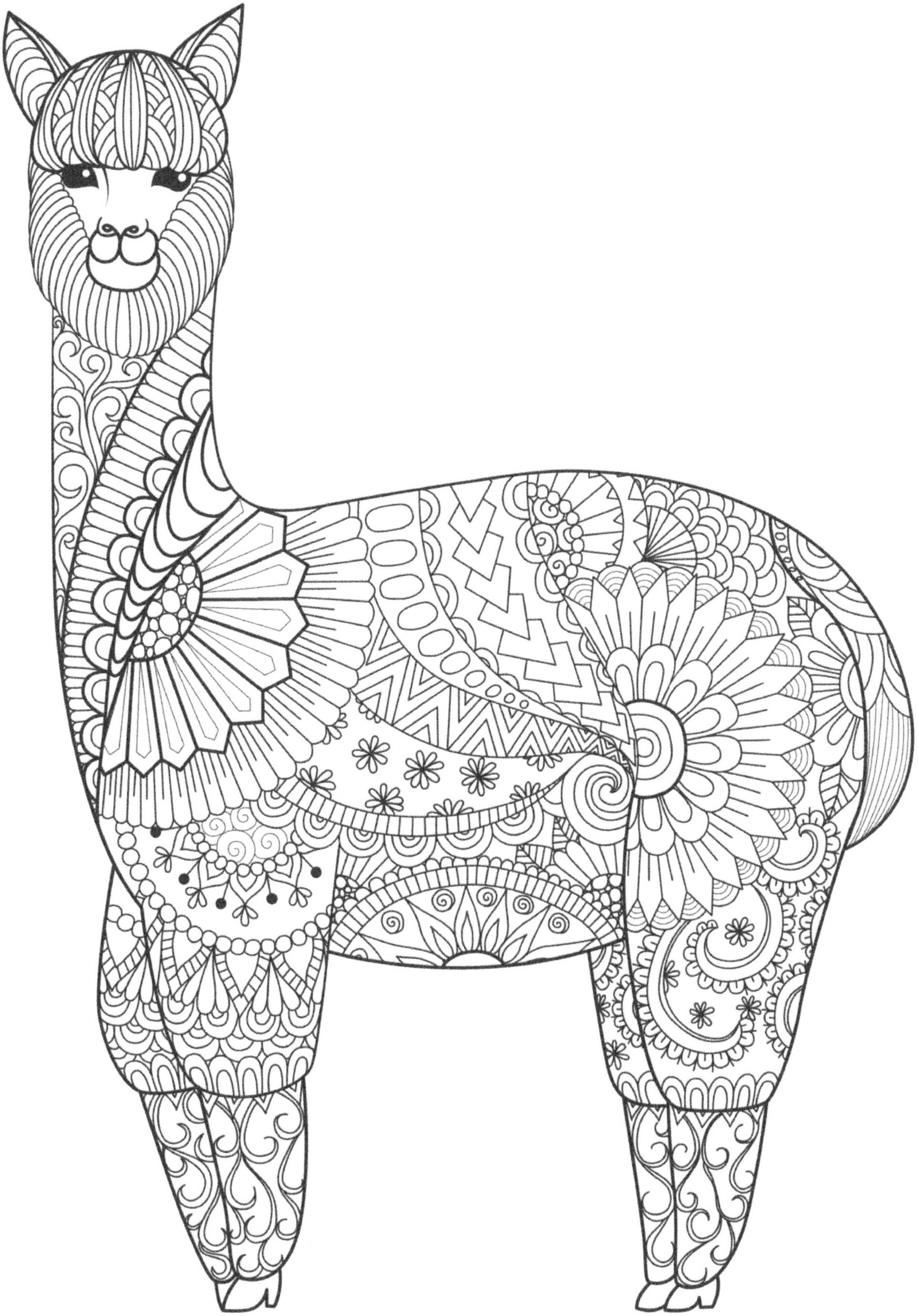

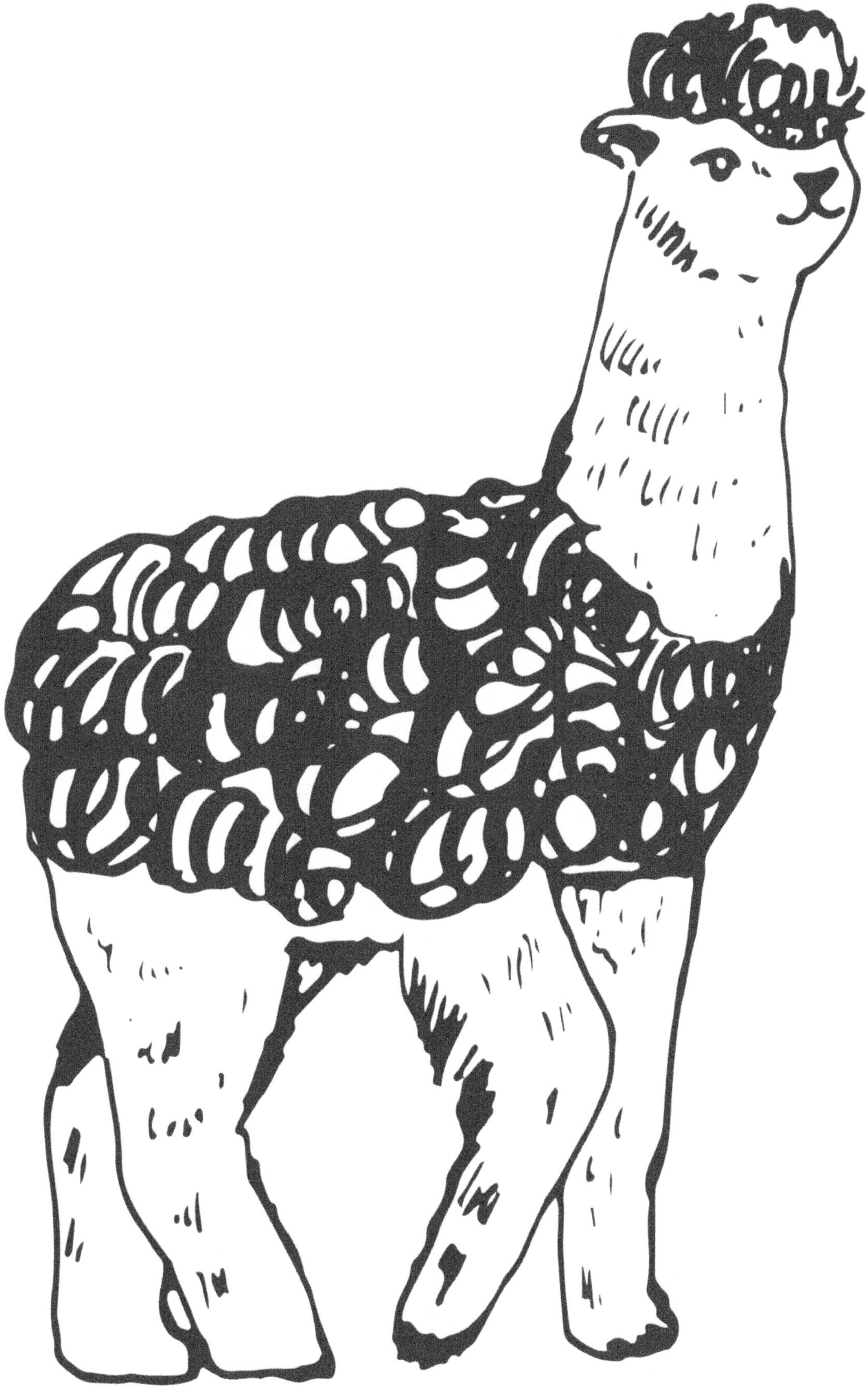

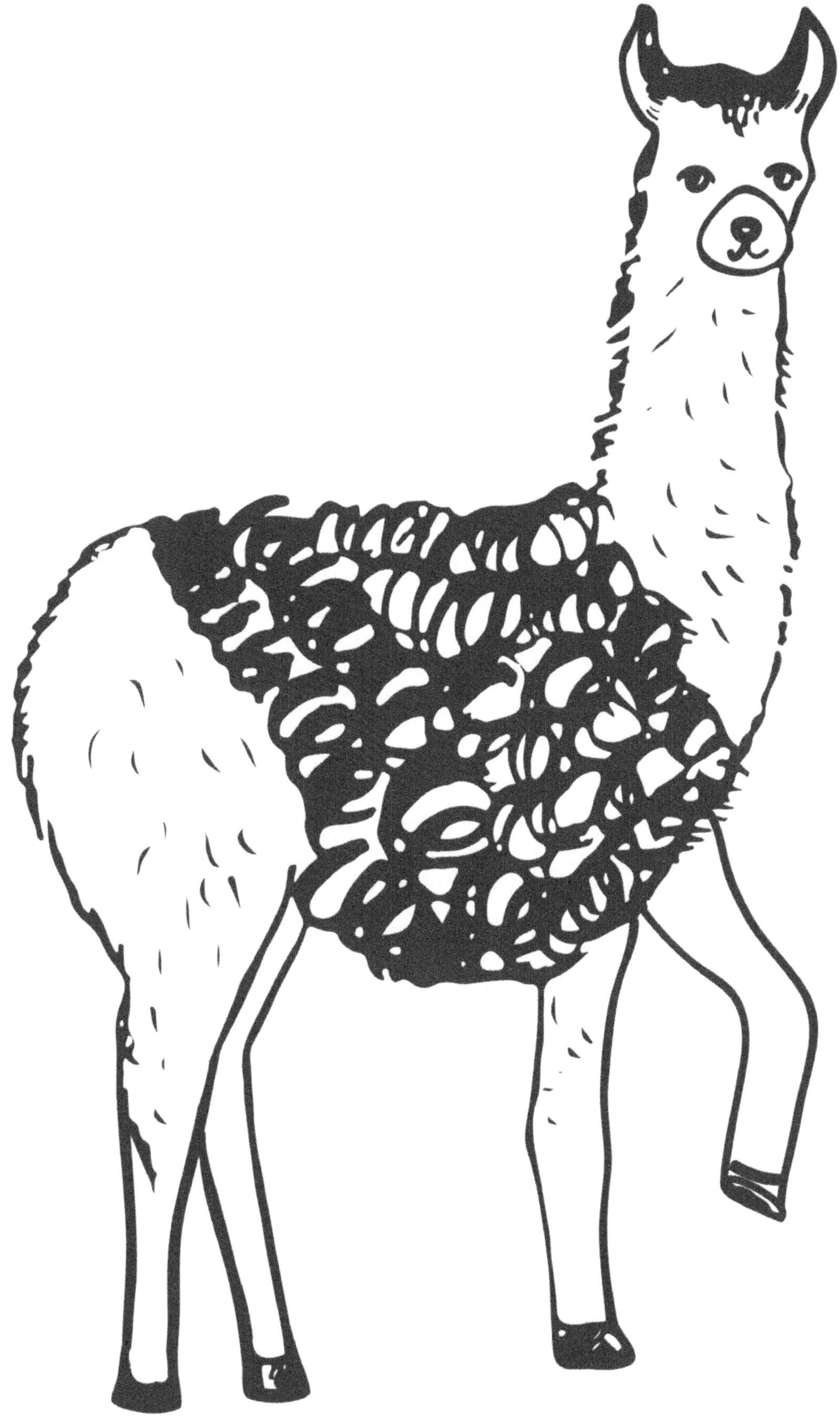

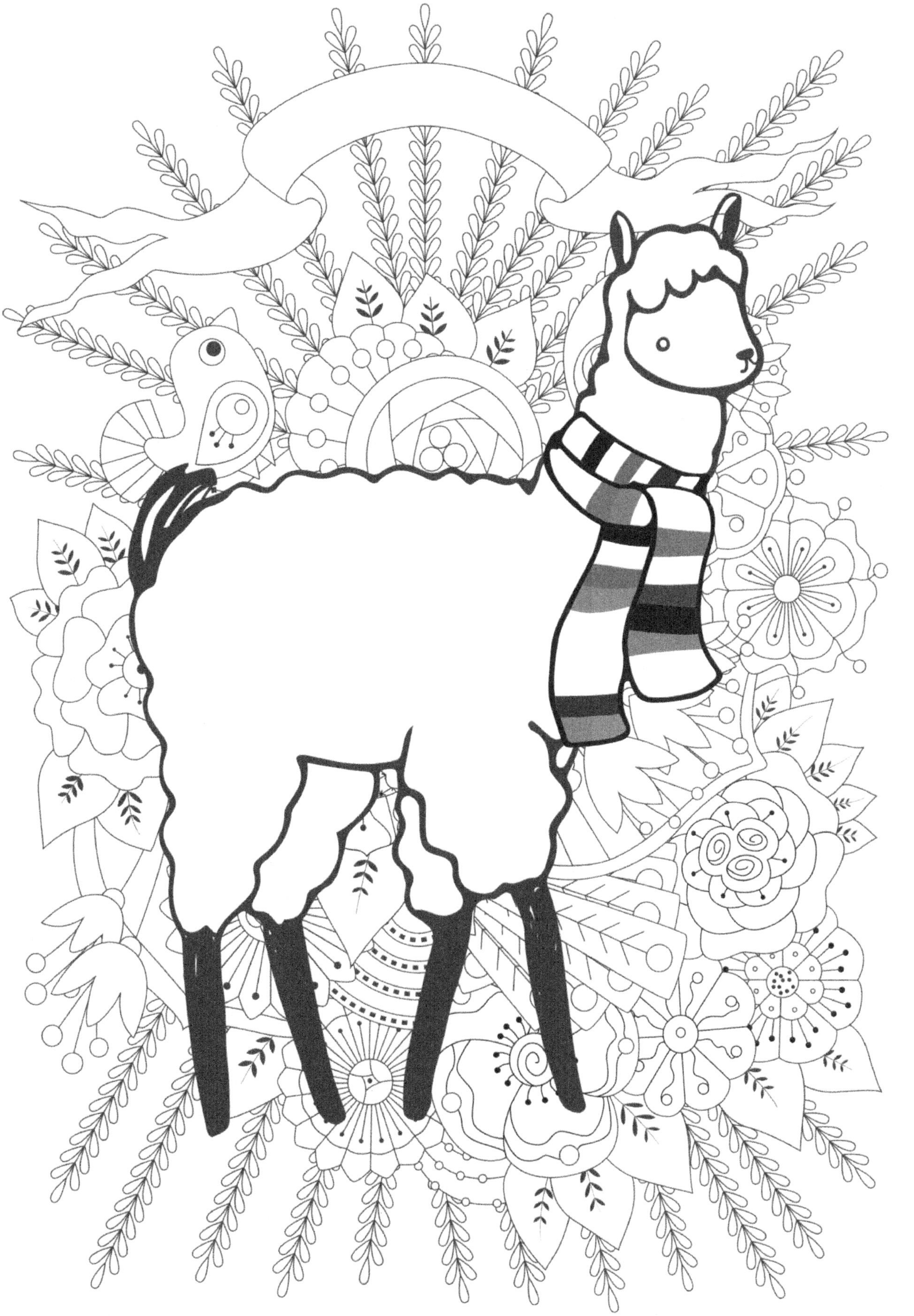

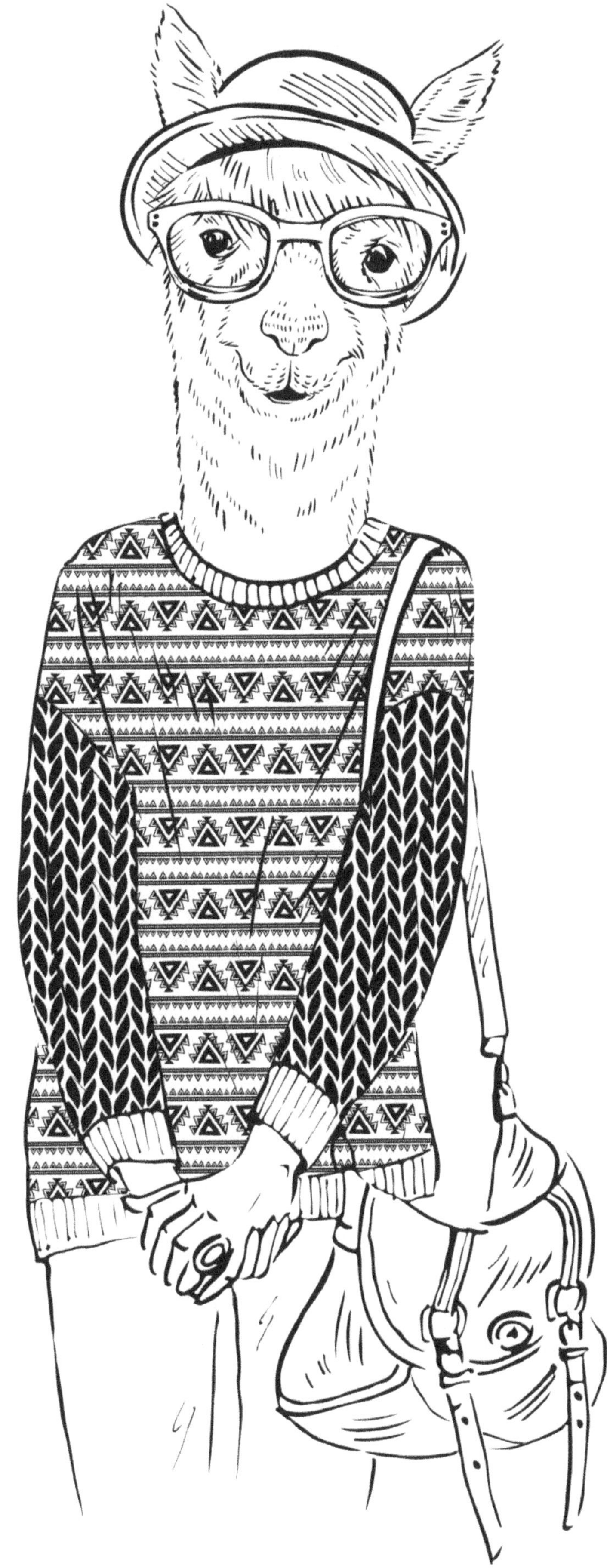

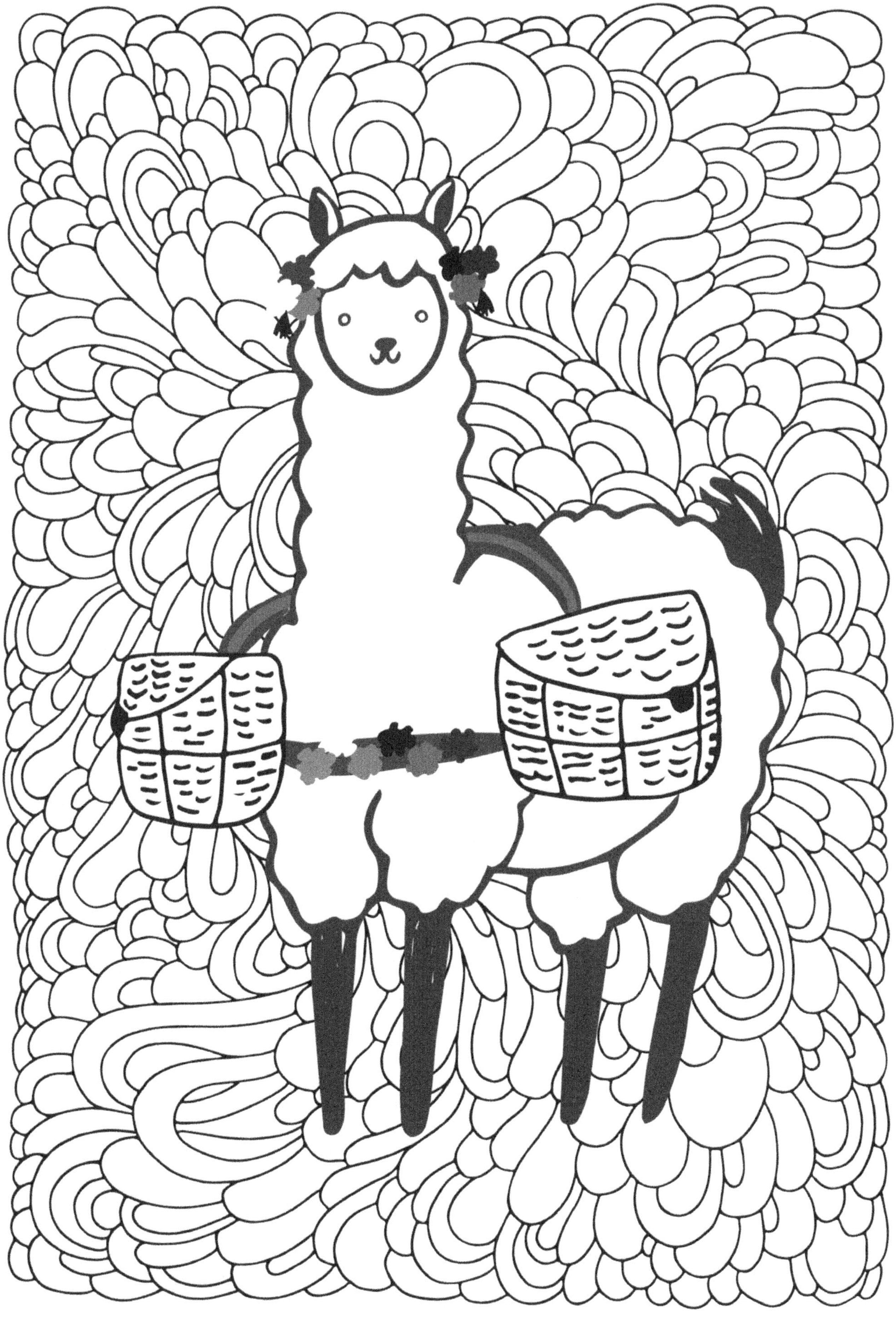

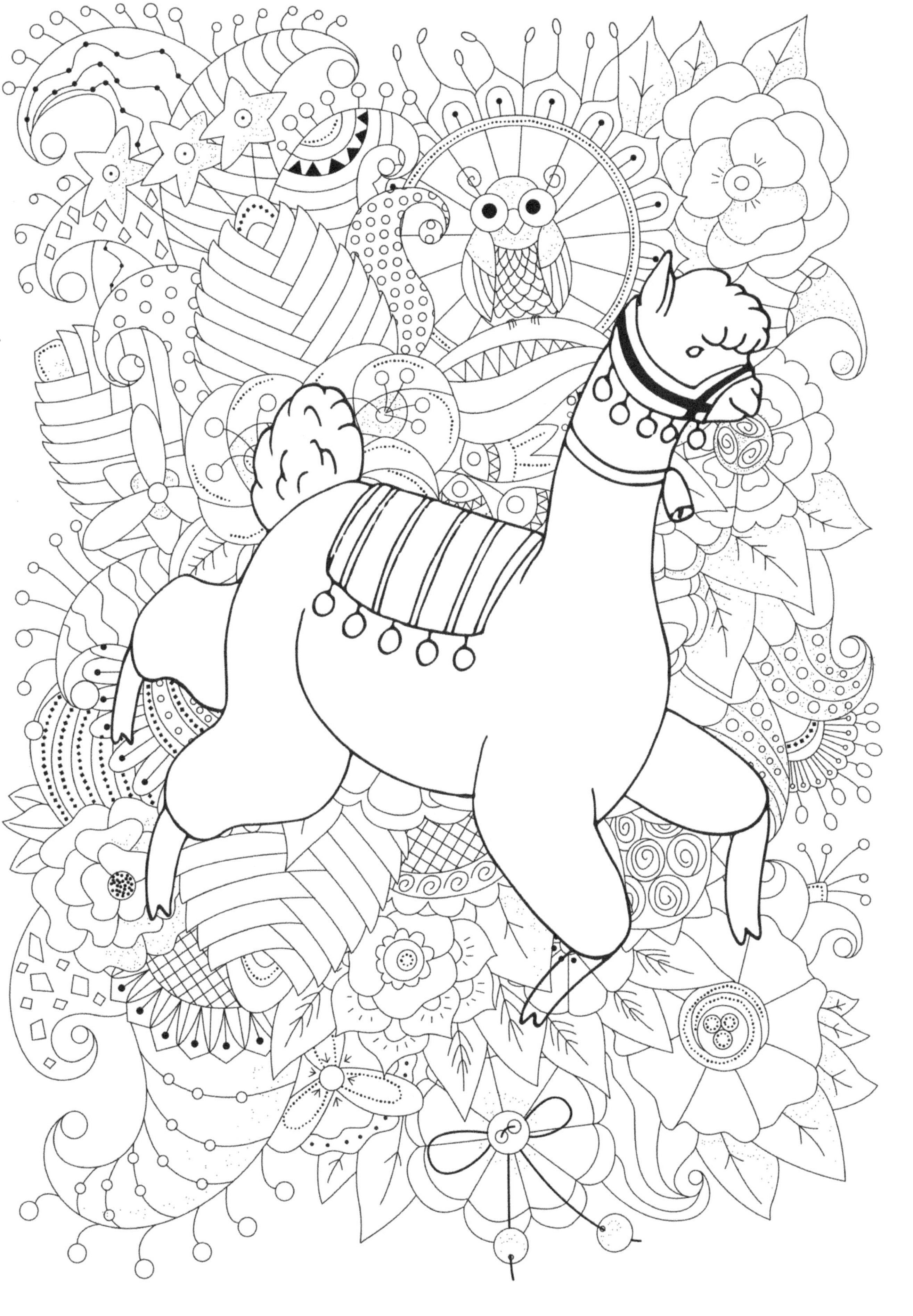

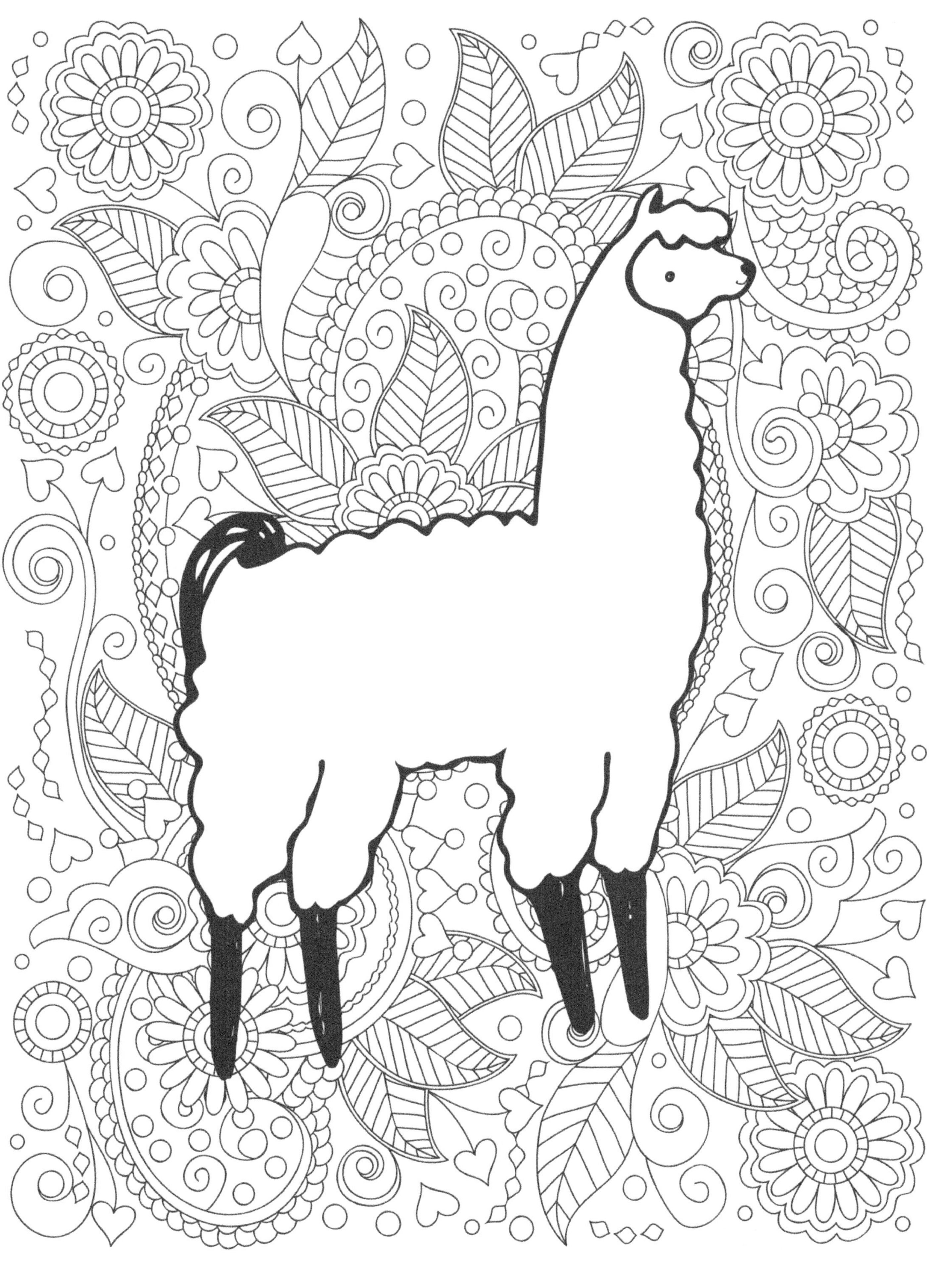

Made in the USA
Coppell, TX
16 February 2020

15857682R10031